Gallery Books
Editor Peter Fallon

LINK Poet and World

Vona Groarke

LINK

Poet and World

Gallery Books

Link (Poet and World)
is first published
simultaneously in paperback
and in a clothbound edition
on 7 October 2021.

The Gallery Press
Loughcrew
Oldcastle
County Meath
Ireland

www.gallerypress.com

ISBN 978 1 91133 822 2 *paperback*
      978 1 91133 823 9 *clothbound*

A CIP catalogue record for this book
is available from the British Library.

Link (Poet and World) receives financial assistance
from the Arts Council.

Contents

Prologue
   To Be Here *page* 11

A to Z 12
'As I dampen the page . . . ' 13
Before 14
'Before he bestirs himself . . . ' 15
Class No. 1: Phrasebook for the Subjunctive 16
'Could you give me some idea . . . ' 17
Daily News Round-up 18
'Detachment . . . ' 19
Evensong 20
'Even on a bus? . . . ' 21
For the Time Being 22
'For a change . . . ' 23
Glissando 24
'Good advice . . . ' 25
Here and Now 26
'Help me out here . . . ' 28
Imagery 29
'I'm aware of your pretty pictures . . . ' 30
Jar 31
'Just say it out straight . . . ' 32
Kist 33
'Kist . . . ' 34
Link 35
'Lounging in the deckchair . . . ' 37
Mystery Set 38
'Music, two kinds . . . ' 39
New York, Hell's Kitchen: Snow 40
'Now listen up . . . ' 43
On Getting Through the Working Day Without Poetry 44
'On the subject of loneliness . . . ' 45
Poetry Manual 46
'Pretend you're me . . . ' 48

Quarantine 49
'Quickly, Irish . . . ' 50
Returning from illness 51
'Right . . . ' 52
Study 53
'Still on the flit . . . ' 55
Trivia 56
'Two glasses of water . . . ' 57
Under a Tree, Parked 58
'Under normal circumstances . . . ' 59
Vona Groarke is writing a poem 60
'Very quickly . . . ' 62
Wall 63
'World sits with his head in his hands . . . ' 64
X = Language 65
'Exactly . . . ' 66
You 67
'You and your . . . ' 68
Z to A 69
'Zenith/doldrum . . . ' 71

Epilogue
    Split Infinitive 73

Acknowledgements 75

Yet everything that touches us, me and you,
takes us together like a violin's bow,
which draws one voice out of two separate strings.
— Rainer Maria Rilke, 'Love Song'
(Translated by Stephen Mitchell)

PROLOGUE

To Be Here

Two bodies to be seen from behind,
arm in arm, stepping into the show.

A face turns, a mouth says one thing
then another is looped through

to fill it out, to glance against,
to miss the point, to nail the nub

and, letter for letter, strut by strut,
to couple. Obviously.

All this to happen here, where you are,
to flex and flinch like so many words

returned as news from out in the world
to where our two fictional bodies link:

my hand in yours; my line, your voice;
what's known to me to be known to you;

one angled sleeve of blue made out
inside one angled black.

A to Z

Almost as if it were real
I make a book of rain
on not the house exactly
but a field across

like news from elsewhere
from over the water,
its seethe and blaze
flocked and bass-lined

until you think enough is enough
and now we will be creatures of water,
our land-lubbing a matter of research
or wheezing anecdote;

us, made over, gilled and silvered
so sleep, when we sleep,
is comparative stillness
while still moving, ruthlessly, on.

As I dampen the page with origin, I see in the shape that water makes the character of World. I will introduce you in due course but, first, some scene-setting.

We find ourselves on a park bench overlooking a steep cliff. The bench has a little name plaque affixed which you can't see because World and I are sitting in the way. World is wearing a claret velvet smoking jacket, in line with your expectations of how he would present himself. Suave. Holding back almost every piece of knowledge he has acquired, but ready to spill it, of course he is, just as long as you know how to ask. He has his I-really-don't-care-one-way-or-the-other look perfected by this time. It's not a look to which you would offer either passion or faith.

World is frightfully good looking in this blue-steeped, liminal light. But, for the sake of honesty, I should say I can't see all of him (who can?): there's a whole other side to his face, for example, I'm unable to make out, sitting alongside him, as I am.

'Honesty?' World says, looking away. 'Really. I'm bored already. I need a drink.'

It's dark, without me noticing the sky having proceeded there.

He gets up. I see how tall he is. How perfectly creased his pants.

'Coming?' he says. (Well, he has to really, or this would be one short book.)

I get up. Now you can see the name.

Except you can't. Of course you can't. It's too dark already.

Before

the moon, like a courtesan at a wedding, slips away before
sunlight colours in its black lines before the first word
gets passed between two people who wake within touch
before the first inkling of rain on slate before the news pips
the hour to significance before today's quota of statistics
shakes out its rude truth before the suck of the door before
the name called before the next drip from the dripping tap
before the chiffchaff drops a berry of song before the day
lowers the rope of itself before the soft whirr of a right
beginning overcomes an evening like the evening before.

Before he bestirs himself, having slept till late, World takes an hour to survey today's news.

He sits up in bed in a house in the country rescued, whitened and simplified (though not, of course, by him). There he decides, as he always does, to live a home-school sort of life with a radio instead of feelings; one stool by a stove.

That lasts until his first coffee. Then it's Go, Go, Go.

The radio says, Come. Bring all your hours in a glass jar with a silver lid and set it down where voices will buff its surfaces with their newest news.

Then remove the lid so an open mouth is a world seen from a window (let's make it a porthole, do) of the International Space Station in today's headline, and a face inside, two eyes and a mouth round as a porthole, round as a world, gawping expensively, fiercely, back at us.

'And?' asks World, dripping coffee on the antique coverlet. 'Your call: what would you have me do now?'

Class 1: Phrasebook for the Subjunctive

Were it not for the glass in the window
    the weather would crowd my mouth.

Were it not for the doorstep
    the hill would crawl under the stairs.

Were it not for the drainpipe
    the rain would hum in my ear.

Were it not for the keyhole
    the morning would not know I'm here.

Were it not for the skylight
    my eyelids would never grow tired.

Were it not for the lit fire
    the world would riddle my breath.

'Could you give me some idea,' says World, 'how long this will go on?'

He's passing a satsuma, hand to hand.

'Somewhere better to be?' I ask.

'Always,' he says. 'But I'll play along for now. Since that seems to be required.'

He tosses the satsuma high. I want to grab it mid-air, of course I do. Instead I watch it fall onto his palm.

'Laid out, end to end, an hour. Tops.'

He nods. The satsuma, I notice, is the only point of colour in this room.

'An hour. That's doable.'

At which point he throws the orange to me.

Do I catch it?

Wait and see.

Daily News Round-up

For another trick (or the same trick,
played out differently), I will convert rain to protest
and protest to everything, making rain,
into the bargain, a kind of everything.

For this I will need the sound of people
and a cause, a reason to be furious
and right. A start point and an end point
(that is nothing of the sort)

and a street or a park
somewhere with cameras and camera-phones
so the march will be picked up and broadcast
spreading from the west or from the east

depending on which way the wind is blowing
and where you stand, this day.
Then it's a question of sound effects,
of turning the volume up or down:

up, to lose yourself in the noise;
down, to hear yourself think,
as if you lived under galvanized
and the rain has news to shake you up

in how it hits the surface, hard,
so hard you think the roof will cave in
but it doesn't: you're still safe and sound
except back there for a second only

when you thought it fell into your name.

Detachment, there's a thing.

You could live in a cottage in the crook of a mountain on the outskirts of a ghost-town and still he will come calling, World, and ask for the kind of herbal tea nobody sells round these parts.

There he is, in the chair nearest the fire, as if he owned the place.

And there you are, glowering, fit to be tied, your right hand spooning the wrong tea into a chipped pot.

'Won't you join me?' says the world. Says World.

And you would, except there's one chair only, and one cup to drink from.

Evensong

Even on a bus home through dark country
with Christmas lights strung town to town,
gatepost to gatepost, shop to shop and every
last door closed, you think, what else is there?
Even if it were not midwinter and the streets
were not telling themselves, time and again,
winter ends, it does, you'd have your doubts

and you'd be right.

You'd as well put faith in the red lamp
in a window of a house elsewise unlit,
see what happens. Nothing, probably.
Unless it's a shadow glimpsed on a switch,
a hand you recognize (with your life in it),
known to put down even those words
that know to give these words the slip.

'*Even on a bus?* As opposed to what — a bicycle? Or skis?'
World has decided to take an interest in my poetry.
He looks me in the eye and says: 'What's that supposed to mean?'

For the Time Being

Call it quits on a night of rain,
excitable rain that fizzes and simmers
as though it's been waiting years to declare
what it has to declare, and gives the world
an imperative and an urgency. All we can do
is marshal attention, allow the day to dissolve,
as it does, in the nothing of our doing
and the nothing we have done.

That this rain hammers itself home
barely needs to be said. In between,
in the half-held breath, listen for
a sideways shift from Chains to Change,
Wrong to Rung, Seethe to Seed
and, eventually, No to Now.

Day will happen, will break, they say,
and when it's done they'll say it has broken
and we (by 'we', I mean, of course, You and I)
will spend it fitting edge to edge, hour to hour
to convince ourselves a pattern is discernible
for betterment, for focus, for the best.

Whether we are there to divine it
or whether we are not.

For a change World is sitting still, stiller even than I.

The room is folded round him like a bolt of cloth being thought of for a suit.

His eyes are closed.

It's possible he's not watching me, but I don't believe it.

'Sitting still for a change,' he says. 'How's that going to work? It's like you thinking something might happen on foot of all these words.'

The room puckers along one seam where the thread's been pulled too hard.

World raises his right hand; to smooth or else to tighten?

It's not for me to say.

Glissando

from the likeness of rooftops
from a shuttered moon
from the lamp in the hall
from a yard of night
from a bend in the road
from a dark blue word
from a silent box
from a restless room
from an open door
from the same door, closed
from a small, low poem
from the huge unpoem
from the middle of
                        whatever this is

                        I music you.

Good advice*

- Believe in me. At least until you find something more worldly to believe in. Then, when you're done with that, come back to me.

- Whatever they say about me is true except this: that I care any more about you than a road does, who's travelling on it.

- That day you spent turning a blanket on the clothesline so every side and corner had its share of sun? That's the day, I tell you, to model all others on.

*(being the heading of the note World has left on my table. The A5, lined sheet it's written on seems torn from an exercise book. He has used a black pen, felt tip, I think, and his handwriting's blocky and determined. He dots every i.)

Here and Now

The day flicks itself on and off
like a cigarette lighter
in a bored teenager's hand.

Reading in creamy sunlight one minute;
the next, the words have darkness in them;
any line much the same as another
in how it sinks or flits.

There have been words —
whole poems of them —
offering various propositions.
(Let's call this 'sunlight'.)

And let us therefore fill the word 'darkness'
with everything else to hand.

Some days I wake to the undertow of a past
I scarcely recognize as mine.
Some days I am weathered by strangeness
and by strangeness I am worn.

So, by evening, the day wants nothing so much
as to chasten me, to bring me to my knees
with its summation of this day's darkness
delivered to my door: the virus mutating,
the daily death toll ratcheting up,
the threat of even more isolation
(is there anything left to be isolated from?).

These days the useful feeling is fear,
the mouldy grain of it under the tongue
to skew my every word, barring the poems.

What if I were to say to you,
Here's one poem about ruination
and another one about hope,
which would you choose?

One, if it helps, is broken walls
and a floorplan just about visible,
clenched between a mountain and a road;

the other is a bowl of water
and the bowl is white.

Yours is not to choose which is which
but to say, This is my choice.

Then to fold up the other one,
half by half, until it's the size of a grain of water
to be dropped by your hand into a lake
from a height determined by you.

'Help me out here, World', I say; 'I tell you so much about myself, won't you reciprocate?'

'Don't kid yourself you tell me things I don't already know.'

'Really?'

'Will that be one of your questions, Irish? I'll give you three, but only because I wish to cheer you up. You cannot live in disappointment. I will not allow it.'

'I don't.'

'That last poem would suggest otherwise. You need to be careful there.'

I can't see any way he's right. Or pinpoint why he's wrong.

Perhaps I could ask him to explain.

But that would be one question down. And I already have so many more.

'How long will you stay?'

'Until I leave.'

He twirls a ring with a red stone around his wedding finger so it snags the light.

'Will you miss me?'

'What do you think?'

One question left.

He takes it off my hands.

He tilts the ring so a droplet of crimson falls in front of me.

'You lack imagination, Irish. See how I draw blood?'

Imagery

If I, wont to plant words in straight lines
as if to make a seam of fritillaries or cowslips,
spend a day (or the guts of a day)
skinning from a low stone circle
moss and sod and all such camouflage
to bring the stones up clean and visible

    (while a robin, so natty I look
    for fob watch and pince-nez,
    gleans behind, oh so efficiently)

then you tell me: what do the stones stand for,
what the moss and what the robin,
in this analogy?

'I'm aware of your pretty pictures, Irish. Of all your many words.'

World is wearing the voice he wears, the sawtooth voice, when he's tired of me.

'I should record yours,' he says. 'Play it back to you, over and over. All its emphases and attentions, like it's combing the language for nits.'

I know World when he gets like this: I decide to play it cool.

'You absolutely do not, Irish. You know nothing at all.'

He turns his back on me. I realize, surprisingly, I'll be sorry if he leaves.

'Of course you will. No audience.'

At least I think that's what he said.

'I wonder you don't wear them out, all these words of yours. They must be resilient. I daresay they'll outlast you and whatever damage you inflict on them.'

'Is that what I do, inflict damage?'

'Why, what would you say?'

'I'd say maybe I inflict meaning.'

World turns round, taps the side of his nose, smiles a little cinch of a smile, says: 'Of course you do.'

Jar

The unused year has been upended like an old jam jar
so all its gee-gaws and mementoes clatter to the floor:
(the time you were due in such a place,
the visit that wasn't, the loved one not seen);
just a few small shiny things once fingered
as if they were, each of them, the Koh-i-noor.

Here they are, strewn just as they fell
with the light of morning (see it now?)
cupping them, their gist and cast,
as if it were a hand on a face
and the face were yours.

I put the jar back where it used to be
before ever I found it for this.
I let it fill it with rain and then
I tip it out again.

Have we found a use for it yet?

Let's place it, for show, up on the high shelf,
call it a jar like any old jar
only perfect of its kind.

'Just say it out straight, why don't you? All this kicking of dirt over, to be frank, not much.'

World has been gardening.

Right now he's got a kneeling pad under his oxter, secateurs in his right hand.

'Weeding?' I ask.

He looks offended.

'Pruning,' he says. 'Try it sometime.'

'I should. I could edit you out.'

World seems on the verge of a smile but then thinks better of it.

'Fact is, Irish, you need *more* me, not less. More me, less you, that is.'

'How much more you would you recommend? More, as in trousers baggier than they need to be? Or more, like a detour? More, like an extra bonbon?'

'Nit-picking, Irish, yet again. The point is, you discard the packaging when you unpack the vase.'

'What if there's no vase, only packaging?'

'Forget the vase. You've got something to say, say it out. Less ornament. Less dress-up. No frill-froll.'

'Sounds like fun.'

'Fun?'

World says it like he's not sure what it means.

'You like dressing on your salad?' I ask. 'A flower in your lapel?'

'With you, it's always more flower than suit. Try that on a cold day.'

'I'll wear the same suit as you do, needs be. The trick is not to pin an actual flower on, but still to have you admire the colour, praise the magnificent scent.'

'I doubt it.'

'Don't. We're actually doing it now, fiddling with a yellow rose, straightening it, just so.'

I fidget with my thumb and forefinger over my left breast.

And World, he just can't help himself, looks down.

Kist

Tall trees are a hymnal even slight winds know by heart,
and stars and traffic, between them, remind me I'm not alone
or at least not any more alone than stars and traffic are.
Mornings are writing; afternoons, repairs. That seems to work.
Nights are a chair for reading about places other than here.
From time to time I open the blue door to ask the world,
What's up? Mostly, the world replies, Oh, you know.
And I do: it could be worse.

I wake in a lean-to bedroom modelled on a casket
with a window at the foot. I prefer to call it a kist,
of course I do, with the knapsack of age-old innuendo
that word carries on its back. Coffin and coffer,
lipped and tongued; the box I climb into
and out of again every time I write a poem.

'Kist,' says World, taking an interest in etymology. 'Where does that come from?'

'Where do any words come from,' I say, 'except from other words.'

'I'm going to need a good dictionary, Irish.'

And then, suddenly, there it is, a thousand-pager, probably, about the size of a headstone.

He licks his forefinger as any child might and sets to leafing through very fine pages I can almost see right through.

'Kist, I've got it!' he says, as if it had been inclined to hide and he'd told it otherwise. 'Old Norse, circa 1300, from *kista*, meaning chest.'

'Well done.'

He gives me his I've-not-yet-finished look, and says: 'And Latin, *cista*, meaning chest. And German *kiste*, meaning chest. Leading perhaps to *keister*, meaning buttocks. Meaning backside.'

He looks up, his forefinger still holding down the word in front of him. If I didn't believe World has seen everything there is to see I'd say he looks offended.

'Meaning *chest* and *arse* are connected via etymology?'

'Yes, World. All linked in.'

I'd say he looks disappointed except how could that be?

He folds up the book as if it were a moth folding its wings together, then lets it open where it will, at any random page.

He moves his forefinger steadily down the list of words.

Something about his progress reminds me of driving through mountain villages. In winter. In darkness. Alone.

'You think there was ever a moment, Irish, when you and I were closer? Or could be?'

'Like that first month in the womb, before the Y chromosome kicks in, when all embryos are female?'

'Why not?'

'Then certainly,' I say.

Link

The cure for loneliness is solitude.

— Marianne Moore

Rooks in the oak quicken on impulse, then flit
all over the place. I swear there's a pattern, if I knew
how to read it, how to breathe in sync. That was earlier,
coming in from the woodshed; now hard frost slicks

the roof tiles under which I try to sleep. I make out
stars I have no name for and the world feels empty
all of a sudden, like the oak when the rooks have,
as if on cue, pulsed once and again, then up and off.

But that's the world for you and no amount of opera
from the Met or thinking of whomsoever you love
or used to do or want to do or cannot sets it right.
And that's before ever you get to rounding on the news

which isn't, would you credit it, so heartening these days.
It's got so it feels like every time I notice the sky
behind the oak, behind the rooks, is a wrong move.
Focus, focus, on what's to hand; on what is in my ken.

It's not much of an answer, granted, but it might be
what I've got and all I need, this fashioning of small rooms
into small civility; into this day's putting of a life on the line
that runs (does it ever run!) from rage to disavowal.

That the times are awkward is known even to a wind
that can turn corners, to a sun that outdoes itself.
And I, fixed between care and nonchalance, all the time
scrubbing off fixity and blanching decency, answer

with finding in a small life a space to breathe, and knowing it
for a luxury, and lining up words, these words, to call it so.

Is this redress or moral failure? Does it fail less uselessly
if I go hard at it, this solitude, determined not to flinch

or buckle, to withstand this day? Fact is, you can't fix
every broken thing. Sometimes the loneliness is too much;
sometimes, it's the hurt. And no answer to the worst of it
but time (which makes everything worse, or seems to do).

And yet. Bulbs do become tulips and snowdrops, and today
is a good day — no rain, no bills, no death to speak of.
If I'm lucky I'll sleep through the night and harm nobody
until I do, which is about all I ask for, these short days.

Lounging in the deckchair World peers over his aviators, says, 'Good luck with that.'

Mystery Set

The wonder is the words stay in the poem
and don't fall off its many surfaces,
sanded and buffed, as they have been,
with silk brushes and brushes of goat hair,
with emery boards and widths of thread,
polished three times before words are set
and then, again, when it is complete.

The wonder is they stay where they're put
without any clasp or tether visible,
each one cut to fit on rails prepared
for a lapidary hand to slip into position
what will neither expand nor warp,
no matter how it is worn or not worn,
laid in a box of darkness, biding time.

You'll have to imagine the before and after,
a head bent over a jeweller's bench; a stand
of callipers, dapping dies, burrs; a leather apron
for scraps or edits; a notion of words against
a white page; openwork behind them open
to firelight or sunlight, whichever, so when
they are most vivid is when they hold most true.

Music, two kinds, a piano concerto and free-form jazz, climbing over each other, skidding in and out, at times so vehement I think if I lie down under it, as under smoke in a house fire, I might just save myself.

And World in the middle, his arms going ninety as if he's conducting the Berlin Philharmonic. Or the Boston Pops.

His face pursed. He's a tightrope walker, and he's wavering.

The piano has the upper hand for as long as it takes him to notice me. Then he turns his back and it's a trumpet telling the room what's what.

And World in the middle, his origami arms folding and unfolding, as if he'll never settle for silence again. As if he's done with speaking to me, and the likes of me.

As if it will have to be full-tilt sound — sound pulled from the space between planets — or nothing.

'I wanted to see if they crossed over,' he says, though I've not asked anything.

He stops moving; his hands, as if someone had switched off the air machine that kept them up and at it, slump by his side.

He turns. He's grinning. He begins to hum.

The sound is like nothing I've ever heard. It's like all the air displaced by the music, every single note not struck, all the breath the dead can't take, all the things I never said when I should have and was frightened to, all the life that was given to me that I made such scant use of.

That: all that.

World, still grinning, still with the deflated hands, says, 'I music you.'

My own words turned back on me.

No escaping them.

New York, Hell's Kitchen: Snow

That year, in the dip of the usual bad sleep,
I opened the shutters on an Eighth Avenue
freshly snowed-on, vacated both directions,
Columbus Circle down to 50th, even Rumour's Bar
in darkness; not a sinner. Not a peep.
And not a window lit, not even mine
even though it was my city then, on loan
or on approval or on tick.

And I had learned the run of it,
the underground shortcut to the library,
where to buy cheap fruit, coffee with taste,
thrift stores; $20 haircuts, dive bars,
a Moorish movie theatre,
the best free views of itself.

I gathered words chalked on curbs:
'Hey Pretty.' 'Trump stole my weed.'
'Jin, John's @ 9.' 'Help me, I'm hungry.'
'You will die too.' And so forth.

I was slipping my hand in the city's hand
and it did not pull away.

The panhandler on 50th and Seventh
would say, 'Good morning, Young Lady'
every morning, and sometimes add, 'Nice coat!'.
(It didn't matter what coat I had on.)

Weekends were films and lattes sitting
in Elizabeth Street or community gardens
with gates you had to close by hand,
maybe a pond with an ancient,
much-loved frog no one has seen.

Weekends were eavesdropping
on the kind of things a city tells itself
when it wants to believe in a future, even so.
Couples in cafes playing with each other's hair.
Students dancing round a fountain to music
on headphones only they could hear.
A small girl in front of a Barnett Newman
saying, 'Hey, that line's not straight'.

I'd save quarters for the laundromat
that was Dublin, down at heel, circa 1982,
except I'd be slipping over the road
to sip pricey cheap winebar Sancerre
while the clothes were in the dryer.

Home again, home again, night after night,
to a lime green room of notionate height,
a marble fireplace and a four-poster bed
I fancied myself Edith Wharton in
and, then, Edith Wharton's servant.
Four brown floors with a brick façade
and a fire escape that used put me in mind
of climbing out some unstrung night
to knock on a door, to knock on a door,
to step over into love.

Well. I put all that in a purple suitcase
with my clam-tight heart and my scratched-at words
to be hauled back down those same four floors
to the taxi's threadbare airport run,
to the up and out and never come back,
to all the struts of the Queensboro Bridge
strumming as I passed, *What if, what if?*

I left when I had to leave, when my time was up.
Brought with me a tin, thrift-store candlestick,
swanky New York shoes, a book I'd written,
a brace of friendships dear to me,
and an aftertaste of hope.

I was young there, it felt like, almost,
on furlough from my life.
And it was kind to me, that unkind city,
taught me lessons worth the learning
about alone and not alone.
Not lessons to be forgotten exactly
but still I'm a diligent student nightly,
practising them in the crook of a mountain
in my converted byre.

Where I too have shutters to fold back
on a dirty night, attending to the weather.
Not snowfall here but wind and rain,
a fire in the stove to countermand them.

And me, wakeful as ever I was,
with rain stabbing the skylight
and not even cars out on the road
but a mountain lording it over the house,
wishful and sullen by turns.

I think myself back to that snow-still street,
my fourth-floor window facing west
(the same west as here, can that be true?)
my breath on the glass, blooming and withering
so it looks like I'm part of what happens,
so it looks like I'm part of it all.

'Now listen up, Irish,' World says, with his back to me.

We are looking down over fields and a river from a height I can't remember climbing to.

'Sincerity,' he says, into the wind. 'Have I not cured you of it yet?'

On Getting Through the Working Day
Without Poetry

The slats of the office blind would have me believe
the deal between me and the world is straightforward.
Turned one way: I am all I need; the other: visit me, please!
Bring a bag with two words printed on it, any two words,
in a line to rhyme with the slats that rhyme with the slats
on next door's door, and with all the slats on all the doors,
the same slats or different slats, depending on how
I codify them and on how you will unpick the code

to read a line about privacy or a poem about desire.
The same words, maybe, but turned fractionally, lightly,
by a hand either mine or not mine, how should I know?

So I cram the space between them with hours

and the day leaves apples and oranges in a bag
to let me know it stopped by.

On the subject of loneliness, World has devised a plan.

'Oh, you're not very good at this,' he says to me, rolling up his sleeves while still managing to signal with one hand the sweep of land between him and me. 'And I suppose you think it's my job now to intervene, to save you from yourself? So many mistakes, I don't have time to count, so much wrongheadedness. Your problem, Irish . . . '

('here we go')

'is wanting always to fill the glass higher than the brim. Even you can see the problem there. So we're going to need a plan.'

At which point World right-clicks into life an over-head projector and computer screen I'd not even noticed there.

He begins.

'Right. Get going. Stir yourself. Write exactly as I say.

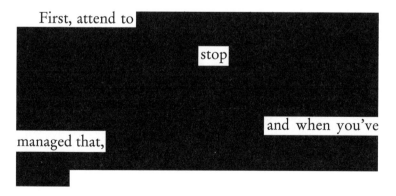

Got it? Let's begin. We've work to do'.

Poetry Manual

1 LONGHAND

One part only of me moving.
The rest of me keeping shtum.

2 EQUIPMENT

My fingers taper to a point.
The nib shows willing.

3 METHOD

Not one bit like keyboard keys,
busy, busy, busy.

4 TECHNOLOGY

One shimmy of a sudden line
suddenly strikes through it.

5 ADD-ONS

The lack of a word-count facility,
of the feint of a change of font.

6 ARCHIVE

Each new poem written off the back of the previous one.

7 SOUNDSCAPE A

Small scratchings like a bird in a thicket. A robin, possibly.

8 SOUNDSCAPE B

My arm across the paper; its slight taffeta shift.

9 PROPOSITION

That ink warmed by my body moves the freer for it.

10 SINISTER

While my right hand is playing with these words
what do you suppose my left is doing?

'Pretend you're me.'

World is doing yoga on a scarlet rug.

'Now? Or in general?'

He shifts onto all fours, arches his back like a startled cat.

I don't like watching World contort himself: it's indecorous.

He has flipped over onto his back, his hands palm down at his sides.

He looks like an oar.

'Or a corpse?' he says. I hate when he does that.

'You've been brushing up on your similes, World.'

'Lowering myself to your level. You're unaccountably fond of a simile, Irish, like a mothballed pantomime horse: mismatched head and tail.'

'Keep practising.'

I'm pushing it.

If he objects he doesn't say so. He curves one arm over his head, lying on his side.

'What am I like now, so?'

A reprieve. I'm on the right side still.

'Squid?' I venture. 'Impermanence? Rain?'

I'm expecting a laugh. Or a tight, wry smirk.

But that's not what I get.

'I don't love you,' he says, his voice veneered so the words slip off. 'Now, what does that feel *like*?'

He's standing with his back to me so I can't tell if he's sore or sour.

So I don't know what he is.

And I don't know what I am.

Quarantine

World dropped by at 3 a.m.
kissed my eyelids, stroked my hair,
said, 'There, there; you're not alone.
I have other calls to make tonight
and every cell of skin I touch
I will ask to remember you.'

And the wind said 'Shush' through the keyhole
and the rain said, 'Hush your lies'.

But I wasn't listening in the least
with my hands brimful of stars.

'Quickly, Irish, pen and paper: I want a record of this!'
Pen and paper, really?
'Quiet, Irish: concentrate. Write every word I say.'
And then he's off: words falling out of him as if he's a dog shaking off a rain shower.

'Cities soft on the inside like fruit going to the bad; townlands that outskirt themselves; countries that shout their names at each other and never, ever stop; rivers calm as footpaths one side of the bridge and fractious on the other; counties that never look in mirrors; fields tilting one way as you walk by in morning, another when the day is done; friable villages; roads with no numbers; hills rubbing up against other hills; parks buttoned up to the neck; lakes with their slate of memory wiped clean; streets with their Sunday faces on, housing estates like honeycombs; parishes turned down at the corners —

— if I had a mind of glass, I would know what to make of it all.'

(Says, 'If I were you, Irish, I'd memorize that — it's not often you find me toying with the idea of limitations.')

(Says, 'If I were you, Irish . . . Which of course . . . ' He stops, smiles his No-need-to-say-anything-more smile, raises an imaginary pencil to an imaginary scribble pad, and pretends, intently, so his brow furrows like a potato patch, to write.)

(Says, looking up, 'Now you can quote me back to myself, hold me to account.' And makes as if to tear up a page, over and over, turning the pieces a quarter-turn each time, ripping them as if they were real, then scattering them over empty ground, like hailstones. Or like ash.)

Returning from illness

                           (an ordinary illness)
as if I'd had my head in the freezer
for a matter of some hours and had seen
(by which I mean cornea, iris. All that.)
a future so stern and bare and cold
I could look only at its black rim
(the ruthless calm, the ice and certainty),

those hours dissolved the heat of my skin,
one and another and another still
all gone, nothing to show for them

but damp sheets and the pillow too
which I, even in fever, had swapped,
to believe a clean start possible
or, if not possible, mine.

And thought recovering from illness
much like returning from love:
the same habit of having to say,
Yes, this is my body: I will live in it.

'Right,' says World. 'This, I'd say, has gone on long enough.'

He surprises me, empathy being about the last thing I expect from him.

'Too long, indeed,' I say. 'Way too long. My eyelids pucker from not being kissed, and my lips from sucking on silence.'

He looks surprised. This I take to be an opening.

'Touch me,' I say, my voice clenched so it won't fray.

'No,' says World, arms stiff as lump hammers. 'It's not allowed. Also, Irish, can we agree that isn't what I meant?'

Study

Matisse's 'Red Studio' to shore up the wall
and a choir to lope through Bach cantatas
in this room I must imagine.
A man I'd have loved to sit at the table,
checking his phone and checking his phone
until I say, I'm here. I'm here.

But let us move past particular love that always,
in the long run, stares us down. A room, any room,
is a way of claiming we've the measure of the world.
We might as well swallow a grain of sand
by way of knowing the sea.
Or say we've hemstitched the horizon
with two threads of sky-blue silk.

And still we fuss about white sheets or cream.
And still we say the stool's in the wrong place
or the picture hangs a smidge to the right
or we'd stay an extra day, if we were let.

I bought a house with holes in the wall,
a roof not inclined to refuse the rain,
meadows in the gutters and cobwebs in keyholes.
Exactly apt, if you see it right,
to balance inner with outer weather,
to keep you in the world.

All of it needed, one way or another:
sun to burn off last night's rain,
birdsong moithering the air,
cobwebs' mezzotinted naves

and me at the mosaic table still

watching spilled tea bait the light
so a bead domes to a hemisphere

thinking, Is this what it is to feel
at the centre of a life?

singing what I thought I heard World sing
when he thought I wasn't listening

> *There, there, Come home by the short road, do.*
> *It's all set out for you.*

'Still on the flit between hither and yon?' asks World. 'There must be a hilltop village in Umbria you've been dying to see? Or a gallery with the only Rembrandt self-portrait you've yet to look in the eye?'

I'm pretty sure he's mocking me. Who goes anywhere, these days?

He's sitting on a huge suitcase I don't think I'd like to lift.

'Exactly,' he says. 'Yet, this is the suitcase you must carry with you on all your future trips.'

'What's in it?'

'Everything interesting that happens here while you are away.'

'Oh, a metaphysical suitcase.'

'I think you mean metaphorical, Irish.'

'If you say so.'

'I do.'

'A burdensome suitcase.'

'That's rather the point.'

He flicks the lock on the suitcase, over and over, so it sounds like a toy pistol going off.

'Why? To stop me travelling? But what am I to do with all this curiosity?'

When he stands up I notice the suitcase, undented, bears no impression of him.

'I don't suppose it matters,' he says. 'Another grey-haired, white woman will be neither here nor there.'

Trivia

Who sits on the grey couch in an empty room? Who reads
by my unlit lamp, flocks cloudy in the mirror so my face
can't be made out? Who leaves my bed as I go to lie down
and scarcely waits for seven bells to stretch out limbs
on sheets warmed by my skin? Whose feet were in these shoes
of mine, damp to the sole though I've not been out all day?
Whose yellow hair is that in the comb; whose blue gloves
where my blue gloves should be? Who sees, now and then,
with my own eyes, speaks with a voice you could lay over mine
and never tell awry? Who thinks as I do, before I do and after,
so my thinking is thinned to a passageway when it ought to be
a realm? Who is it answers to my name, rises from my skin
and bones to account for me? Who climbs clear of my life
this morning, out through the skylight in mid-air, off into
purblind, public yonder, not to be seen (or not by me) again?

Two glasses of water filled to the brim, and World with a hand hovering over each of them.

'Your job today,' he says to me, 'is to transfer the water from each glass to the other without spillage and without using your hands, your mouth or any third receptacle.'

Receptacle: that's World for you. He still has that dictionary.

I love a challenge as much as anyone, but you might as well ask me to breathe, I think, without using my body.

'In which case,' says World, reading my mind, 'you might want to question your usage of the words *you* and *your*.'

Ah.

'Close your eyes,' I say.

He does. He really does.

I count to ten, I say each of the numbers.

'Open them,' I tell him. '*Et voilà!*'

'You didn't do it,' he says.

'Prove it,' I say.

He withdraws his hands.

And then the glasses are somehow empty.

And I feel an unaccountable thirst.

And I'm crying.

There's a surprise.

Under a Tree, Parked

The rain has so much news to impart
it taps on the sunroof and slaps on the glass
and tries its hand at Morse Code, once,
but quickly tires of the subtlety
and shunts to bass-line facts.

This rain seems to be always saying,
'Oh, and another thing',
all its stats and certainties
like shouting in the room where you are
and nowhere else to go.

Jabbing, pinching, full of itself,
this rain insists it be listened to
as if it had the answers, yes,
to every empty question rattling
in this vacant afternoon.

There is no talking back to it.

I am out in the world
and the world is happening
as small stones thrown, repeatedly,
right over my head.

I am tight against it, it would appear;
breathing in what I breathe out
and nothing in between.

'Under normal circumstances . . . ,' World begins, then seems to cut himself off and, after finding his Take-it-or-leave-it smile, proceeds: 'You can have that one for free. It might prove useful, presently.'

His little joke.

'Thanks,' I say. 'I've got it.'

Because the writing of this has to be mine.

'Like you get to do the divvy-up,' he says.

I hate when he does that.

'As I was saying, *under normal circumstances*,' his voice with the sharp edge facing out. '. . . we'd need to be working up to some sort of goodbye.'

'These are not normal circumstances?'

World stands up, joins his hands at the crotch, rolls his thumbs around each other, thinking, as if he's been petitioned to judge a particularly sticky case.

'The answering of that,' he says, 'would be a damp note on a triangle in the silence between spheres.'

World is not often enigmatic. But I choose not to be scared.

From another room comes the sound of pecking. Or pipping. A five-second blip.

An alarm establishing it works. Or a bird on a windowsill. Or fingers tapping on the drum of the world.

'Like news?' he asks.

He's ahead of me.

'Like news,' I say.

He laughs.

And then I'm scared.

Vona Groarke is writing a poem

and it's not going well.

So much world to be acknowledged,
so much to be refused!

How many ways can rain be turned
to something more than rain,
or the thin sticks of the alphabet be asked
to shore up a life lived glimpse by glimpse
and not much undertow?

Such high hopes! Such wanting
to get in everything that matters
these strange days: virus, meanness,
hopelessness, all that.

A world in disarray.

Against it, what we have to hand,
hope and anger criss-crossing the page.

Look, look at the screed of notes,
the clumps of print-outs, the strike-throughs!
There's the rack and screw
on which the poem confesses or is lost,
and there, right there, is the warp and weft
of the poem she wants to craft.

Which is very different, yes, from the poem
she's crafting now.

But she meant well, allow her that,
intending to make of one small poem
a space as large as it needed, really,
to be adequate.

That it proved also wide enough to fall through was, heigh-ho, *unfortunate*.

Knowing her, she'll try again.

What else would she do?

Very quickly, World decides to abandon interest in my poetry.

'Though I quite like that last one, Irish; how you pull yourself every which way in it. And how you make it clear that 'you' means me.'

'Do I?'

But he has said all he has to say and so busies himself, as usual, with leaving.

Having zipped up his brown leather boots, next World pinches his trousers into a neat front crease.

'The next world?' he says, straightening. 'Is that what you just said?'

He seems eager, as though I've made him a promise, which I don't believe I have.

'No, you can't have, Irish. I must have misheard.'

Which might be the first time I've ever heard him admit to a mistake.

'How can there be a next world', he says, 'when there is but me?'

Wall

A breeze-block wall, ugliest thing you ever saw,
the day has yet to dawn that would brighten it
or the moon to rise to grace it. That wall needs
another wall, of fuchsia, maybe, or cotoneaster,
something giddy and chatty and blithe
to fill in all that gloom and drag
with flighty schemes for what a wall might be.

That wall needs to not be a wall,
to set aside the fact of itself
and then to become a whole other wall
dreaming itself up the back of the mountain
sinking bits of itself in ditches
as if they were gobbets of monkish gold,
or shedding all straight lines and angles
as if to be a stream.

Leaving the remains of it, the underside,
the seething absence
(look closer — worms, silt and so on)
where last I saw it
end-stopped and awfully sure of itself
nothing much now,
even less than when
it pegged its tuneless certainty
to the limit of what's mine.

Nothing much? Try nothing at all
but grass clumping where an edge used to be
and swaying into the white space
either side.

World sits with his head in his hands and will not look at me.

'Something I did?' I want to ask.

But it's always something I did or didn't; something I said or forgot to.

And if it wasn't World taking me, this time, blamingly, to task, then it would be World next time.

Or the time after.

Or the time after that.

$X = Language$

Y
=
the
feeling
and
the
not
feeling
and
what
all
comes
between

'Exactly,' says World. 'For once, Irish, I agree with you.'

He is busy seeming to measure something in blocks in front of him.

One two three, go his hands. One two three again.

'What are you doing?'

He looks at me, focuses, looks down, looks up; makes to hand me an invisible box about as wide as he is.

And I extend my hands to take it.

Because what else would I do?

You

Under normal circumstances one would pull
from the heart of all this rain
a name, dry to the touch,

dry as a silence tended and turned, daily,
to the windowpane
so all its surfaces get even light.

Under normal circumstances
all its jags and about-turns
would even themselves out

to a straight line
connecting me and you
and everything between.

But tonight your name coheres
into the place where you should be,
the body you should occupy,
the voice snatched up from the street
and dizzied to a question
asked, specifically, of me.

And me, I can't help myself,
I pin all sense of time
to its rough, anxious edges,

take in my two hands my self and,
as if it were a page on a spike,
I pull my life down tight over your name.

'You and your You,' says World. 'Your indeterminate but always obligingly faithful You, You You You You You You You You You You You You You You You You You You You You You' (with every word, he blinks, again), 'You You You You You You You You You You You You You You You You You You You You You You You You You You You You You and You.

'Have I forgotten anyone?' he says. 'Oh yes, You.'

Z to A

That was how it worked, you see:
the long and short, the in and out,
the through and through of it.

Daylight was for moving forwards,
night-time, for undertow: a book
to be read, a chair to call home,
a laptop open to news of news.
Those after-dinner hours being
for being in tune with the world,
indeed, and also most alone.

Which is better? Which, most forgivable?

I go back and forth on it as if in scripted dialogue
with the other character in my life, the chatty,
full-on, made-up one (who has to look, of course,
like me — that we might catch each other's eye
and be, rightly, terrified).

What I want is to be asked a question
I don't have an answer to
so instead, I'd touch my lower lip
as if to dust off all my words
and sprinkle them in a little heap
I and my speaking self would step over
as we leave the room.

And yes, I must always be leaving a room
having looked inside and clocked no ask
to which an answer, fully-formed,
was not lying in wait.

So, World, world, with your news like rain
relentless, disaffected,
bored with itself;

World, world with your rain like news,
as if for me only to open my door
to its ritzy promises; to surrender outrage
and/or complicity; to be, briefly, absolved;

World, what would you have me do?
I listen, turn away, turn back.

I choose to live between these facts;
to find each of them likewise unhelpful
and both of them equally true.

Zenith/doldrum; pith/gist; zeal/lull; chains/change; World/
poet; (Can you tell who's speaking now?) backroads/
inroads; catch/cinch; here/herd; list/listless; news/nous;
orange/no orange; rain/rain; silence/anything but.

EPILOGUE

Split Infinitive

to meadow
to lantern
to muslin
to linnet
to morning
to fingertip

to anvil
to rafter
to gatepost
to adze
to minaret
to yonder

to opal
to sepia
to anymore

and to alone

to heartily alone

Acknowledgements

Acknowledgements are due to the editors of the following publications where some of these poems, or versions of them, were published first: *Agenda, Hudson Review, The New York Review of Books, Poetry Ireland Review, The Poetry Review* and *The Times Literary Supplement.*

Thanks to The Gallery Press (as ever); to Van Cleef & Arpels for a residential fellowship at the wonderful Bogliasco Foundation in October 2019; and especially to Colette Bryce, Kia Corthron and Conor O'Callaghan for their careful and wise advice about this (admittedly) quite odd manuscript.